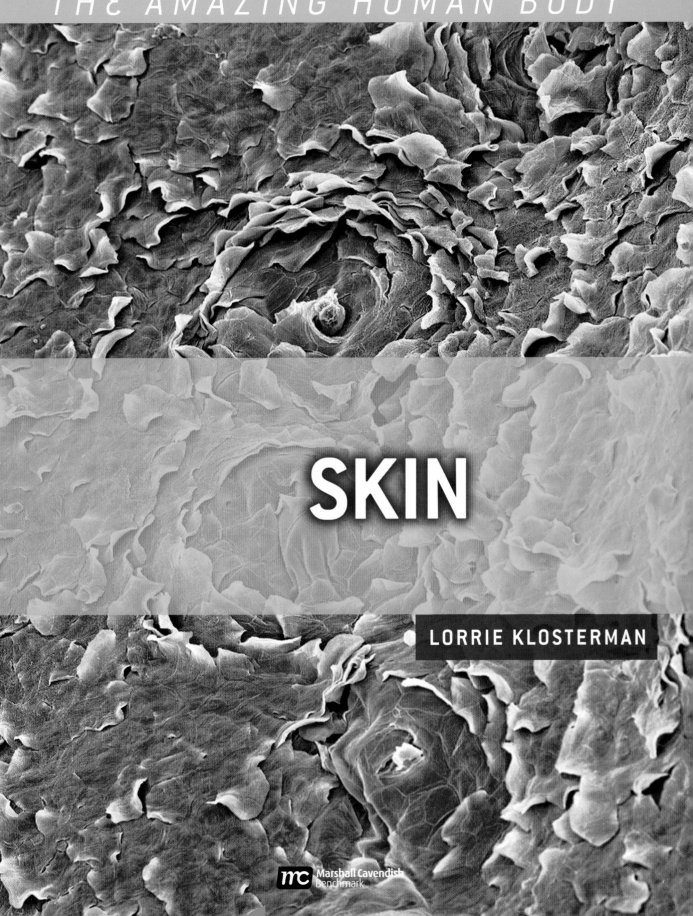

THE AMAZING HUMAN BODY

SKIN

LORRIE KLOSTERMAN

Marshall Cavendish Benchmark

Marshall Cavendish Benchmark
99 White Plains Road
Tarrytown, New York 10591
www.marshallcavendish.us

Editor: Karen Ang
Publisher: Michelle Bisson
Art Director: Anahid Hamparian
Series Designer: Kay Petronio

Library of Congress Cataloging-in-Publication Data
Klosterman, Lorrie.
Skin / by Lorrie Klosterman.
p. cm. -- (The amazing human body)
Includes bibliographical references and index.
Summary: "Discusses the parts that make up human skin, what can go wrong, how to treat those illnesses and diseases, and how to stay healthy"--Provided by publisher.
ISBN 978-0-7614-3057-5
1. Skin--Juvenile literature. I. Title. II. Series.
QP88.5.K56 2009
612.7'9--dc22
2008017580

 = collagen, a major component of skin

Front cover: Epidermis
Title page: Sweat glands
Back cover: Collagen

Photo research by Tracey Engel

Front cover: Photo researchers, Inc. Andrew Syred
Shutterstock: William Attard McCarthy, 4; Emin Kuliyev, 14; Marilyn Barbone, 15; iofoto, 27; Michael Sheehan, 33; Rob Byron, 44; Suzanne Tucker, 57;Tootles, 60; Elena Elisseeva, 62; Robert Pernell, 64; Aleksandar Vozarevic, 66; Sandra Rugina, 67; Cathleen Clapper, 68; Brian Chase, 69; *Alamy:* Nucleus Medical Art, Inc., 6, 48, 52; Peter Arnold, Inc., 7; Maximilian Weinzierl, 8; Blend Images, 11; PHOTOTAKE Inc., 16, 24, 26, 38, 65; Medical-on-Line, 19; Adrian Sherratt, 20; imagebroker, 22; Stefan Sollfors, 28; ICS, 30; Martin Jenkinson, 35; Engima, 39; Pavel Filatov, 40; Danita Delimont, 41; Image Source Pink, 42; Ecce Inc., 51; Janine Wiedel Photolibrary, 54; mediacolor's, 55; WoodyStock, 70; *Photo Researchers, Inc.:* Steve Gschmeissner, 10, 25; James Stevenson, 12; BURGER / PHANIE, 13; SPL, 1, 23; Lauren Shear, 32, 58; Pascal Goetgheluck, 34; John Burbidge, 36; Mike Devlin, 45; Antonia Reeve, 46; CNRI, 47; Phanie, 49; David M. Phillips, 50, back cover; Biophoto Associates, 56; Dr. P. Marazzi, 63; *SuperStock:* Image Source Black, 18, 29.

Printed in China
123456

CONTENTS

1

What Is Skin?

When you think about important parts of the body, what comes to mind? Perhaps the heart, or the brain? Or maybe the stomach, or the eyes? It is likely that most people would not mention the skin. Sure, our skin has some interesting features, such as freckles and moles, and it comes in a variety of appealing shades. But besides that, the skin is pretty boring, right?

The truth is, the skin is just as important as the heart, brain, or any other more "famous" part of the body. It has many life-sustaining jobs. One is creating a boundary between ourselves and the world around us—a boundary that helps to keep us free of germs and chemicals that might make us sick. Another of the skin's jobs is holding in moisture,

The skin and all of its structures that form the body's protective covering—such as hair, glands, and nails—make up your integumentary system. The name comes from the Latin word integumentum, *which means "a covering."*

so that we do not dry out. Additionally, hair, nails, sweat glands, and oil glands are part of the skin.

The skin is made of two portions. One portion—the surface that you can touch and see—is called the epidermis. The other portion is underneath that, and is called the dermis. These portions are quite different from each other, but they work together to carry out the skin's many jobs.

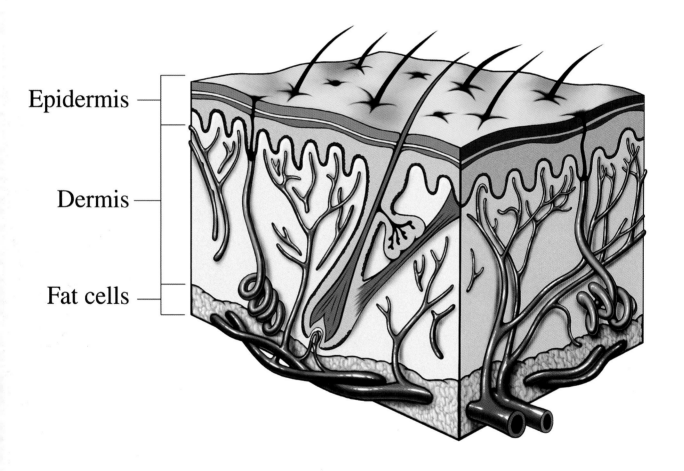

Epidermis —

Dermis —

Fat cells —

The epidermis and dermis have specialized structures that help with important body processes, including protecting the body, maintaining normal body temperature, and aiding in sensory reception.

COVERED IN LAYERS

Have you ever had a sunburn that later peeled off in thin, pale flakes? Or maybe you have noticed that in dry weather, tiny flecks of skin rub off your arms and legs? If you have noticed these, you have seen evidence first hand that the epidermis— the skin's outer portion—is made of very thin layers. Each layer is too thin to be visible. But hundreds of layers are stacked up on one another, adding up to something visible.

These layers are made of cells. Cells are the smallest living things. Our bodies are made of trillions of cells, of which there are hundreds of different kinds. Cells in the epidermis are very flat. Each is attached to its neighbors, so that a single layer of epidermal cells is like a patchwork of fabric pieces sewn together to make a bed sheet. In addition, the cells of one layer are stuck to the cells in the layers above and below them, like having many patchwork sheets glued on top of each other.

Though we have been comparing a sheet of skin to a bed sheet, a bed sheet

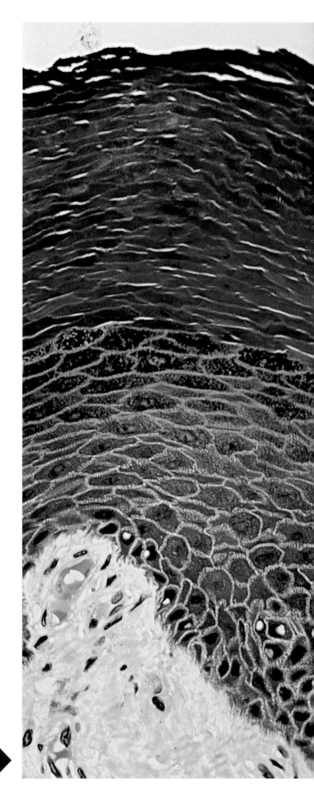

Magnified at one hundred times its normal size, this skin sample shows the many cell layers that make up the epidermis (bright purple). The lighter, pinkish area below is part of the dermis.

cannot repair itself if it is torn, or grow larger to fit a larger mattress. But skin can. Cells in the skin are able to make copies of themselves to replace damaged or dead cells, and to make additional cells that will fit over a growing body.

Fingerprints and Creases

Skin looks like a fairly smooth surface, but just pick up a magnifying glass, and you'll be fascinated by the textures on your skin. It has lots of ridges, creases, and pores—a real microscopic topography. Fingerprints are the best-known surface feature of skin. You can easily see them through a magnifying glass, or by touching something colored, such as a warm

Fingerprints are a combination of whorls, arches, rings, and ridges. Prints like these can also be seen on your toes.

chocolate bar or an ink pad, and then pressing your fingertips onto white paper. The rings and whorls of lines that show up are your fingerprints (toes have them, too). Notice that your fingers' prints are probably different from each other. A person's ten-fingerprint set is unique: nobody will have that exact same set of patterns (though a few people may have something similar). Fingerprints are with you for life, even though the epidermis cells of fingertips die and fall off continually. It is the skin's dermis, below the epidermis, that sets the pattern. Serious damage to the dermis is the only thing that can alter the pattern. Even a deep cut does not do much but create a line through the remaining pattern.

Creases in the skin, easily visible to the naked eye, are present on the palms, soles, and at joints, such as the inside of the elbow. Additional creases develop over a person's life, at places where the skin is regularly folded or bunched. Lines in the face, due to smiling and frowning, are good examples.

SKIN CELLS: LIVING AND DEAD

Skin is one of the few places where it is good to have dead cells. In fact, dead cells are what make skin such an excellent covering. Within the epidermis, several of the outer layers—those at the body's surface—are dead. As we go about our daily activities, the dead cells get bumped, rubbed, and scraped off. You can see evidence of this by putting a piece of transparent tape onto the back of your hand or arm. Then pull it off gently and hold it up to the light. You'll see that the tape is not transparent anymore! It has captured dead skin.

Of course, if dead cells were to come off without being replaced, the outer layers soon would be gone. Fortunately, the epidermis has layers of living cells below the dead ones. The living cells continually make new cells, which push older cells toward the surface of the body. The older cells die and get rubbed off.

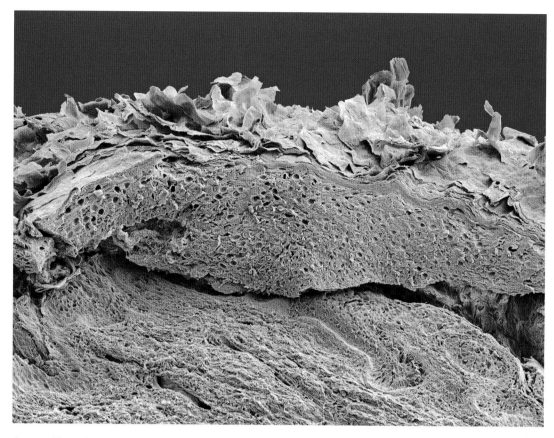

A magnified slice of healthy skin shows how the uppermost layer of the epidermis—the stratum corneum (shown here as light brown flakes)—is made up of keratinized cells that are constantly dying and falling off.

Skin cells are filled with a protein called keratin. The cells make the protein when they are still living. Because the skin's epidermal cells are good at making keratin, they are often called keratinocytes (-cyte means "cell"). Keratin helps to make skin tough and waterproof. Hair and nails are also made of cells packed with keratin (as are the feathers of birds, scales of reptiles, and claws of many animals).

A variety of other cells are nestled among keratinocytes of the skin's epidermis. Some of the living cells help to fight off germs that work their way beneath the outer layers of skin. Other kinds of cells help us feel things that contact the skin. A general term for this kind of cell is a sensory cell—it senses, or notices, something about the world around us. Sensory cells in the skin allow us to notice such things as a tiny bug tickling our arm, or the soft feel of a kitten against our cheek. Sensory cells work with other cells, located just below them in the dermis, to send signals to the brain about what we are touching.

SKIN COLOR

We all have seen that skin can be different shades of tan, brown, or beige. The color is due to a kind of cell nestled in the epidermis that makes pigments, which are colored substances. The pigment in skin is called

Skin color is determined by the amount of melanin produced by a person's melanocytes. How many melanocytes a person has is usually determined by heredity, or the traits passed down from parent to child. But even within a family, shades of skin color can vary.

BIRTHMARKS

Most people are born with some markings on their skin. Some of these markings are simply areas where the skin is a different shade than surrounding skin. Other markings have blood vessels within them, or may be raised above the skin's surface. The most common kinds of markings are birthmarks, moles, and freckles.

Birthmarks are present when a baby is born, or show up soon afterwards. Birthmarks that have extra skin pigment, or coloration, look brown, black, or bluish. Those that have blood vessels in them look reddish or pink. Some kinds of birthmarks have their own names. For instance, "port wine stains" are deep red or purple because there are many blood vessels that make the mark look like the color of dark wine.

This young woman was born with a large birthmark on her leg. Laser treatments performed by a doctor can help reduce the size and lighten the color of the marked skin.

Moles are a very common type of birthmark. They may be flat, but often are a raised bump. They can darken with age, so they become noticeable as a person gets older. Moles are usually small and harmless, though sometimes they can be a place where skin cancer starts.

Freckles are spots, too, but they are flat, plentiful, and are usually light brown in color. Some people are born with freckles that never go away, while other people only get them temporarily after being in the Sun.

Nobody really knows what causes these skin features, but they help each of us to look unique. Sometimes, though, a mark may be large enough to be annoying or embarrassing. In that case, a doctor can usually help by removing it or reducing its size.

melanin. The cells that make melanin are called melanocytes. Melanin can be dark brown, reddish brown, or yellowish brown. The different shades combine to give various shades of skin. For instance, someone whose cells make both a yellowish and a dark brown melanin will have more of a bronze color than a person who makes just dark brown melanin. Skin color also depends on how *much* melanin the cells are making. A lot of melanin makes dark brown skin, while a small amount of melanin makes pale skin. People with a rare condition, albinism, do not make melanin at all. Their skin is very white (as are their hair and eyes, which would normally contain melanin, too).

One of the children in this family has albino traits. Unlike her parents and siblings, she lacks melanin.

As a baby grows, his or her skin color can change.

The color and amount of melanin in a person's skin is inherited. Which means skin color is passed down from parents to their children. However, if parents have different colors of skin, their children have a blend of the two colors. If one parent makes a lot of melanin and has dark skin, and the other parent makes only a little melanin and has light skin, the children make a medium amount of melanin and have medium-brown skin. But just as children of the same parents can look different from each other in many ways (unless they are identical twins), siblings—brothers and sisters—can have different shades of skin color. One child may be fairly dark-skinned, while his sister is lighter-skinned.

It can take a while for a newborn baby's skin to get good at making melanin. Because of this, some babies of dark-skinned parents look paler than their parents for months. But these children become darker as they get older. On the other hand, some older people are paler than they were as a middle-aged adult.

PINKS AND TANS

A suntan is a temporary darkening in skin color caused by sunshine. It happens because the melanocytes react to the Sun's ultraviolet (UV) radiation by making more melanin. Also, the keratin in the skin's layers darkens a bit. Freckles get more noticeable with Sun exposure, too. Freckles are spots on the skin where melanocytes are grouped together (some people are born with freckles, others get them in reaction to the Sun).

Sunburn is a reaction to too much UV radiation. The skin has been irritated, its blood vessels widen, the skin turns pink, becomes tender, and may form blisters. Flakes of dead skin that were burned may peel off days later. People with pale skin usually burn more easily than they tan. This is because they have less melanin. Frequent or very bad cases of sunburn can damage the skin enough to lead to skin cancer. That is why sunscreen, sun hats, and limiting one's time in direct sunlight are recommended for everyone, even those with darker skin.

Some freckles darken in the Sun, but fade after a while.

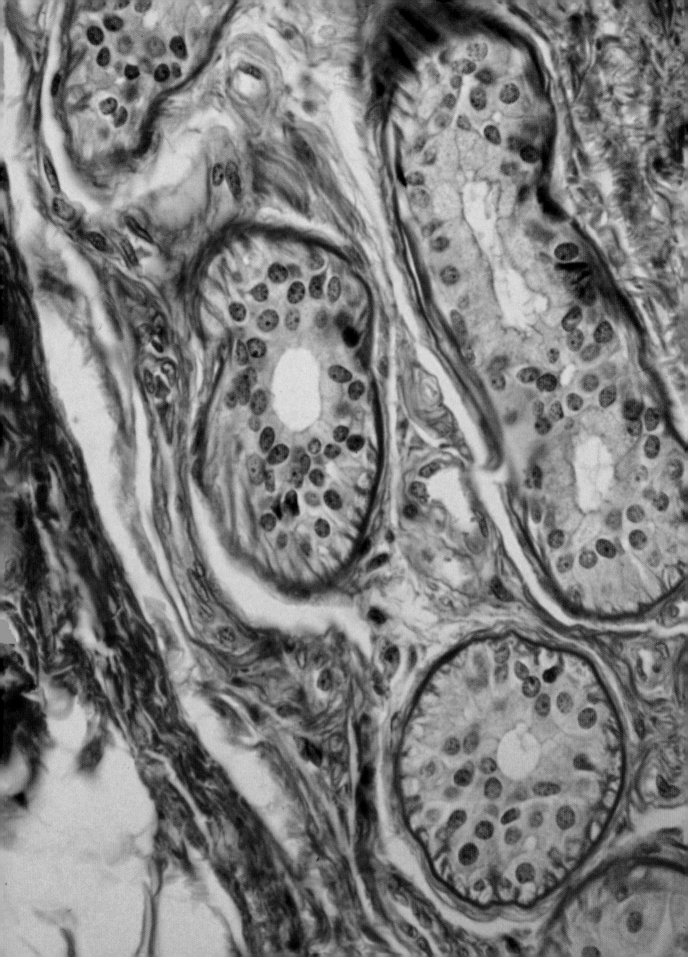

2

The Dermis: Secrets Beneath the Surface

The dermis is quite different from the epidermis, though you cannot tell that without the aid of a microscope. Only when samples of skin are magnified many times—and are viewed much larger than their real size—can the secrets to the skin's construction emerge.

Unlike the epidermis, cells in the dermis are far apart from each other, with a lot of room between them. Some of the cells appear to have long narrow "arms" that extend out in many directions, touching their distant neighbors. The cells are called fibroblasts because they make tiny fibers—threadlike strands—that course through the dermis. Among the fibers are substances that hold water—like a sponge does—

This is a magnified view of sweat glands, which are located in the dermis.

which helps to keep the area moist. Mixed in with the water are nutrients, oxygen, and other life-sustaining materials that continually drift among the cells, keeping them healthy and active.

STRETCH AND STRENGTH

When you bend your knee, the skin over it stretches. When you straighten your knee, the skin returns to its unstretched shape quite well. This ability of skin to stretch and return to its shape is called its elasticity. It is like the elastic around a waistband, or like a rubber band, which can stretch, then recoil, or return to original size.

The skin is elastic because of tiny fibers in the dermis called elastic fibers. They are made of a special kind of protein called elastin. These fibers give most of the stretch-and-recoil quality to skin. (Many other parts of the body are elastic, too, thanks to elastin fibers, such as muscles, the lungs, and the stomach.)

The skin is not just elastic, but it is also very strong. Imagine all the things your skin goes through in a day. It gets rubbed, squished, stretched—and usually survives just fine. And while the layers of epidermis give the skin some of its toughness, the dermis gives the skin its greatest strength. The material responsible for this is called collagen, a type of fiber made of protein.

Collagen is a very common "building material" throughout the body. It gives strength to many internal

Collagen can be found in different parts of the body. The collagen in the skin is arranged in a meshlike pattern that helps to give skin its strength.

organs, from muscles to bones to blood vessels and nerves. Collagen fibers are much larger and tougher than elastic fibers, and they do not stretch very well. But in the dermis, collagen fibers are arranged in a crisscross, or meshlike, pattern, like a net made of threads. This allows the dermis to stretch a bit in all directions. Thanks to collagen and elastic fibers of the dermis, it is easy to see why the skin is often compared to a living fabric!

KEEPING SKIN ALIVE

Blood vessels are plentiful in the dermis portion of skin. (That is why scrapes and scratches bleed, even if they are not very deep.) Blood brings oxygen, food particles, water, vitamins, hormones, and other essential substances to every living cell. These substances seep out of the tiniest blood vessels and enter nearby cells, including those in the living layers

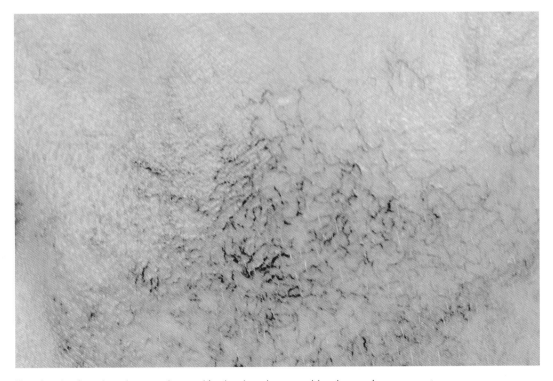

Despite the fact that they are located in the dermis, some blood vessels are easy to see.

BLUSHING AND FLUSHING

Have you ever felt a sudden warmth come over your face when you are embarrassed about something? Maybe you had to give a report in front of the class at school, or you knocked over a water glass at a restaurant. That warmth is because tiny blood vessels beneath the skin get a bit wider for a few minutes, bringing a bit more blood to the face than usual. Because blood is red, the skin gets pinker, too. This reaction is called blushing, and it is a very common, natural response to feeling embarrassed or self-conscious. People with dark brown skin may not look like they blush, since the red color does not show up as easily. But they do.

Another similar color change of the skin is called flushing. This means a sudden reddening of the face and other places such as the neck and chest. As in blushing, the color comes from the blood vessels widening and bringing more blood to the surface of the body. A person might flush because they are very hot, or during vigorous exercise. Some medications may make the skin flush, too. In most cases, blushing and flushing end after a short period when the blood vessels contract and go back to their normal size.

Increasing your heart rate—with emotions, by running, or doing some other physical activity—makes blood rush to the vessels near the surface of the skin causing blushing or flushing.

of epidermis, which have no vessels of their own. But the outer layers of epidermis are too far away from blood vessels to get all they need to stay alive. That is the main reason the cells on the surface of our bodies are dead.

AN INFORMATION NETWORK

The dermis has a large network of nerves running through it. Nerves are the body's rapid communication system. They are bundles of extremely long, thin cells that carry signals between virtually all areas of the body, spinal cord, and the brain. This system is called the nervous system. Nerves can be compared to electrical wires that carry electricity throughout a house. In the skin, nerves send information to the brain and spinal cord, such as how warm or cold the body's surface is, where things are pressing against the skin, and if cells are being injured. With this information, the brain makes decisions about what to do.

We make hundreds of decisions each day, thanks to this skin-brain and skin-spinal cord communication. Examples are putting on a jacket because it is cold out, quickly pulling your hand out of water that is too hot, getting the dog off our lap when it is too heavy, and smacking at a mosquito that is biting.

SWEAT GLANDS

Sweating has something of a bad reputation because of advertisements that sell antiperspirants (products that attempt to stop sweat from forming in the armpits) and deodorants (products that cover up smells in the armpits). These ads suggest that sweating is an ailment. But normal sweating is a natural process that helps cool off the body. Sweat is mostly water, and as it evaporates, it takes some of the body's excess heat with it. And sweat itself does not have a bad smell. Whatever unpleasant smells

Sweat comes out from tiny pores on the surface of the skin.

may be associated with it are made by bacteria living on the skin. These bacteria use tiny amounts of nutrients in sweat to survive. The bacteria then release chemicals that can have bad smells.

Sweat is made by tiny groups of cells, called sweat glands, located in the dermis. There are sweat glands on nearly every inch of skin. Each gland releases a moist secretion through a pore (an opening) to the skin's surface. The sweat glands under the armpits, and also near the genitals, are somewhat different than the rest. Their sweat has fats and proteins in it that bacteria can use. These types of sweat glands are not fully working until puberty, which is when boys' and girls' reproductive systems start to mature. Then, the sweat glands develop more fully. This is one reason why antiperspirant and deodorant use does not usually occur until around the teenage years.

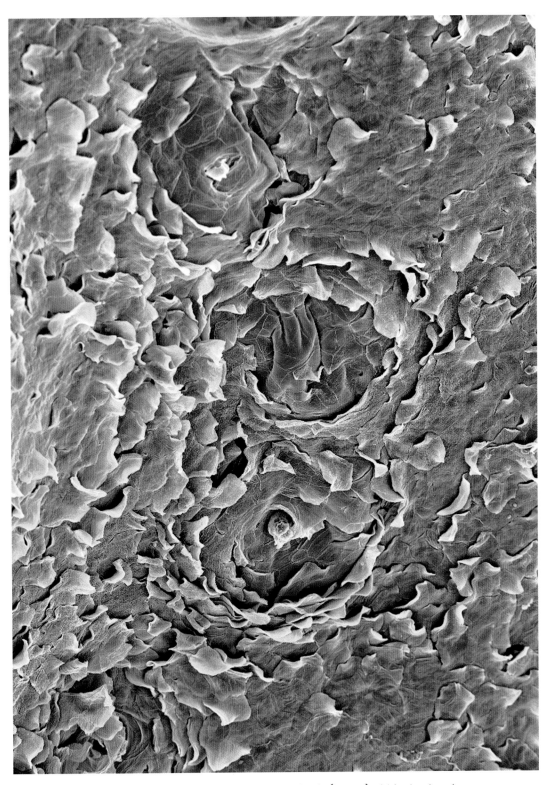

A colored scan shows a magnified view of three sweat glands (green) within the dermis.

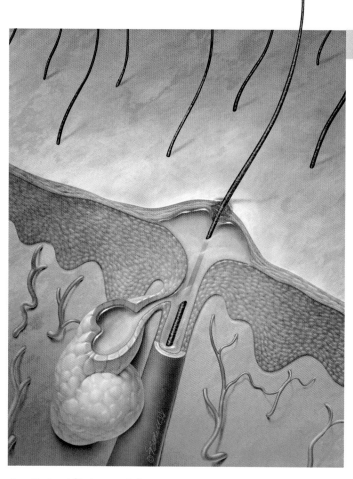

An oil gland (light purple) secretes oil out of pores. Oil helps keep the skin healthy, but a build up of oil (yellow) in the pores may cause infections.

OIL GLANDS

The dermis is also home to oil glands. These tiny groups of cells make an oily liquid that gets onto the skin's surface through a pore. Oil glands are most noticeable on the face, neck, chest, and scalp. There are no oil glands on the palms of the hands and soles of the feet.

The oil helps in waterproofing the skin, and it keeps down the number of bacteria living on the skin. Many oil glands share a pore with a hair that springs up from the skin. The oil helps keep the hair flexible instead of dry and brittle. Like sweat glands, oil glands become more active with sexual maturity.

HAIR

Many animals have fur, hair, or feathers over much of their bodies. Beneath all that fur and feathers is skin, from which the hair or feathers grow. We do not have fur or feathers, but we do have hair over most of our bodies, too. It is plentiful enough in some places that you can see it easily—for example, on your head and near your eyes (eyebrows and eyelashes). During puberty, hair becomes more visible under the arms and around the genitals, and on the face and torso of men.

But a good deal of our hair is so fine that it is hard to see. With a magnifying glass, though, you can see that it is everywhere. Each hair comes out of a small pore in the skin's surface. The hair is made in the dermis. There, a group of specialized skin cells called a follicle are busily making new cells. The cells are packed with keratin and firmly stuck to each other. As new cells are continually made, the older ones die and are pushed out of the follicle through the pore as a long, thin strand. That is the hair. There are melanocytes in the follicles, too, which make pigments that get into the hair and give it color. As a person ages, less pigment is made, until eventually none is made at all. Hair without pigment looks white.

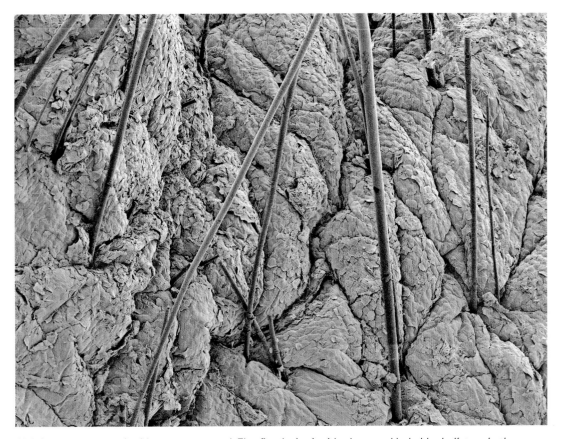

Hair is even present inside your ear canal. The fine hairs inside the canal help block dirt and other substances that can damage the fragile structures inside your ear.

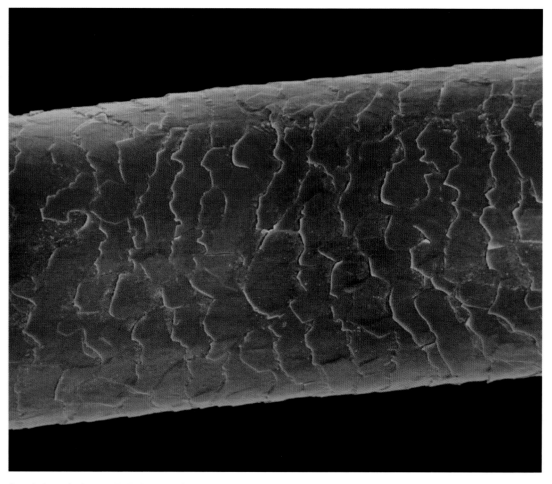

Tough keratin layers help keep hair strong.

Hair is quite a remarkable structure. Keratin is very tough material, and the cells are so well linked to each other that hair can withstand months, or years, of washing, combing, and rubbing. Of course, hairs fall out. The average person loses up to a hundred head hairs each day. Eyebrows and eyelashes fall out too, though less often. The reason hairs fall out is that every so often, each follicle takes a rest. The living cells stop making new ones for several days or weeks. During that time, the hair falls out. Soon, though, the follicle gets busy again and starts making a new hair.

You may notice that some hairs are short, as in the eyebrows, while head hair gets to be quite long. The difference is due to how long the follicles are busy before they rest. A follicle that is active for a few months before resting will make a shorter hair than a follicle that is active for years before resting.

NAILS

Fingernails and toenails are also made of skin cells packed very tightly together. If you look at a fingernail, you will see a pale, crescent-shaped area near the base of the nail—the end opposite the fingertip. That pale area is the lunula (meaning "little moon" in Latin). The lunula is where living cells are busy making the nail by continually producing new cells.

Even though they are harder and look different from regular skin, nails are made of the same materials as skin.

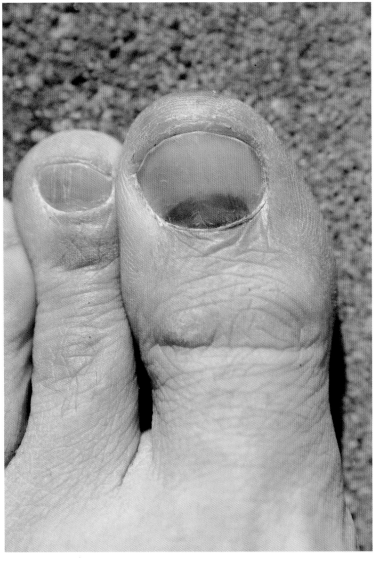

This person has stubbed his big toe, injuring blood vessels beneath the nail. As the nail grows out, the bruise will fade and eventually disappear.

As the cells fill with keratin and get tightly packed, they move their way out to the fingertip in a sheet. That is the nail.

Nails grow very slowly. If you ever accidentally hit your nail hard, a white mark will form on its surface, or a reddish-brown mark beneath the nail may appear where blood leaked from an injured vessel. As the nail grows, it will take weeks or months for these markings to reach the tip of the finger.

Some people have had the painful experience of injuring a finger or toe so seriously that that the nail area turns bluish-black, due to blood that has collected under the nail. Usually the nail will fall off in a few weeks, because the cells that make the nail were badly injured and need to recover. In a few months time, a new nail will emerge and slowly grow to proper length.

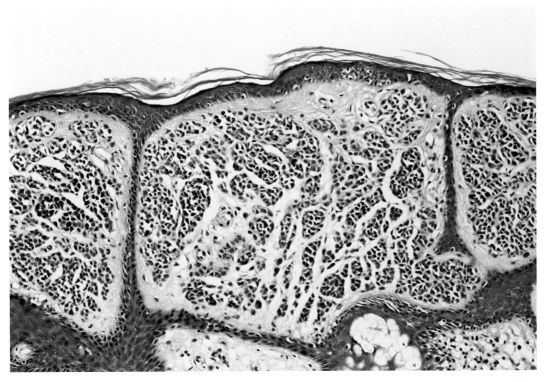

This is a magnified sample of skin. Skin is made up of many different components and may take different forms. Without your skin, hair, and nails, however, your body would have a tough time functioning.

WORKING TOGETHER

The skin is a lot more complex than it seems at first glance. The epidermis and dermis are quite different from each other, but they work together to make many substances and structures found in the skin—or sticking out from it. Together with the bloodstream and nervous system, the skin is able to carry out many different tasks that are essential for life.

3

The Skin's Special Jobs

he skin helps to give each of us a unique appearance. Its many shades and markings, such as freckles, moles, and perhaps scars, give us a certain look. Hair, which is made by skin, is very important to outward appearance, too. But besides the role skin plays in our appearance, it does many other things that are essential to life. Some of them we hardly ever think about.

PROTECTION FROM INJURY

Nearly every living thing has some way to protect itself from the world around it. The skin is part of this protection for many creatures. The

Goosebumps form when muscles at the base of a hair tighten. The hair stands up and the skin forms a little bump. Strong emotions such as excitement or fear can cause goosebumps, but they may also pop up when you are cold.

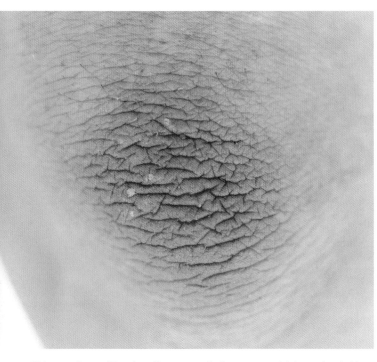

Skin on places like the elbow usually have more folds and wrinkles because the skin there is thicker.

thick fur or hair that covers dogs, cats, and many wild animals allows them to frolic in the outdoors without getting easily scraped by every twig or stone they encounter. Humans, on the other hand, can get scratched more easily. And yet, human skin is still quite sturdy most of the time. And think of all the wear and tear your elbow, knees, palms, and soles of your feet go through! In those places, skin is especially thick and tough, and a good protector.

PROTECTION FROM DEHYDRATION

If our skin were just a thin layer of cells, we would quickly dry out. That is because anything that is moist—like our insides—can lose water by evaporation to the surrounding air. That is why wet clothes will dry when they are hung outdoors, and why rain on a sidewalk vanishes soon after the Sun comes out. It is also why certain animals, such as frogs and salamanders, are at risk of drying out and dying if they stay too long in dry air. Those creatures have a thin skin. And though humans are just as moist inside as frogs, very little of our moisture can get past the skin's many layers of keratin-filled cells.

Of course, the outermost layers of skin sometimes get dry and flaky. This happens especially during cold winter weather, or in climates that

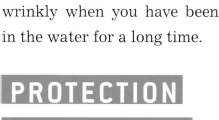

are dry and hot. In these circumstances, the small amount of moisture in the skin's outer layers evaporates into the air. On the other hand, if you soak in bathtub or go swimming for a long time, the outer dead layers take in some of the water. That is why fingertips look puffy and wrinkly when you have been in the water for a long time.

PROTECTION FROM GERMS

Skin is an amazing organ that can both absorb and repel some substances, such as water.

One of the skin's most important jobs is keeping out germs—bacteria, viruses, and other microorganisms that can make us sick if they get inside the body. The skin protects against germs in several ways. First, it is a physical barrier, meaning that germs simply cannot get through it. Bacteria, which are especially plentiful on everybody's skin all the time, are kept on the surface where they usually do no harm. The skin also has a thin layer of acidic moisture made by sweat glands, which is harmful to microorganisms. In addition, oil from the skin's oil glands keeps bacteria numbers low.

But sometimes the skin's outer layers are broken through, such as when you get a cut or a deep scrape. Germs can then get into the dermis below, where they can harm living cells. Germs can also enter the bloodstream and travel throughout the rest of the body. This can make a person very sick. Fortunately, the body is well equipped to tackle such invasions. It has

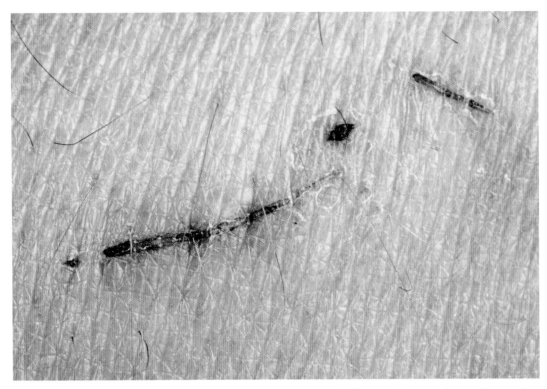

Scabs, which are clumps of clotted blood and other substances, help to seal cuts and scratches on the skin. Scabs stop the bleeding and prevent germs and dirt from entering the body. With time, the skin begins to heal and the scab eventually falls off. Picking off scabs can reopen a wound, cause an infection, or cause scarring of the skin.

a whole collection of cells—the immune cells—that specialize in finding and destroying germs. These cells are part of our immune system. Immune cells are found virtually everywhere in the body, including in the skin— both in the living layers of epidermis, and in the dermis.

The skin is an excellent place for immune cells. They can stop germs that have entered a wound from getting much further. How? For one thing, immune cells can destroy germs. They also send out alarm calls, in the form of chemicals they release, which attracts additional immune cells to the injured area to kill off germs. (Sometimes, though, a doctor's attention and medications are needed to help the immune system get the job done.)

PROTECTION FROM HARMFUL CHEMICALS

If it were not for the many layers of dead skin cells, some of the substances we handle every day could injure, or even kill, living cells below. Even plain water, or soapy water, would injure living cells. In this way, the epidermis keeps us protected from any liquids or chemicals we handle.

Still, some substances can work their way across skin, into the dermis, and then into the bloodstream. Those substances tend to be ones that mix well with oils, such as gasoline, turpentine, alcohol, certain cleaning products, and many liquids used in manufacturing. Toxic metals such as lead and mercury also can penetrate the skin. Many of these substances can make a person very ill, or even cause death. So it is important when handling chemicals to read all safety information about them. Use protective gloves and clothing if warnings say to do so, and always wash your hands afterward.

Chemicals like fertilizer and pesticides can be dangerous if they are absorbed by the skin. People should always wear proper protective gear when handling dangerous substances.

PROTECTION FROM RADIATION

Skin keeps much of the Sun's ultraviolet radiation from getting to deeper parts of the body, where it could damage internal organs. Melanin, the skin's brownish pigment, is a good UV absorber, meaning that the radiation that hits melanin stops there. Keratin, too, absorbs some UV radiation. Skin gets better at blocking UV after Sun exposure, because the radiation causes melanocytes to make more pigment and keratin to darken. Both of these reactions make the skin look darker, or "tanned," after sun exposure.

However, UV radiation can harm the skin cells themselves. That is why everybody who is going to be in the Sun for more than about fifteen minutes should use sunscreen or sunblock, which have UV-absorbing chemicals. They stop much some of the UV radiation before it gets to the skin. Hats and light clothing should also be worn to protect the skin.

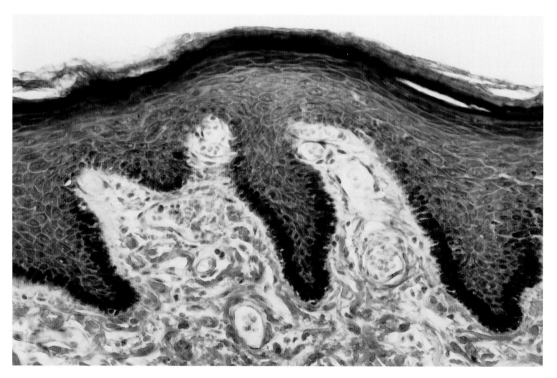

This skin sample shows the dermis (light blue) and the epidermis (darker layers). The darker layers have many melanocytes that produce melanin. Melanin can help prevent some damage by UV rays, but everybody should wear sunblock or sunscreen when spending a lot of time in the Sun.

MAKING VITAMIN D

Even though people are encouraged to wear sunscreen, the skin needs some sun exposure—10 or 15 minutes a day—to make vitamin D. Scientists have found that living skin cells make vitamin D when they are exposed to UV radiation. (Actually, the skin makes an unfinished form of the vitamin, which must then travel in the bloodstream to be finished by the liver or kidneys.) Vitamin D is necessary for a healthy body. It allows us to use the calcium in food. Calcium is an essential ingredient of bones. In addition, all living cells use calcium in a variety of life-sustaining activities. Many of us do not get direct Sun exposure each day, especially in the winter in the north. But vitamin D is also present in foods, so that can help us get enough.

SENSATIONS

Have you ever seen a book for young children that has things to touch—soft, rough, sticky, smooth? At each turn of the page is a different item to feel. These books are a delight not just to children but to older people, too. Most of us cannot resist feeling the texture of something that looks interesting. The skin also tells us whether something is cool or warm or dangerously hot. It perceives pressure against the body, too. All of these sensations are part of the wonderful sense of touch.

The sense of touch brings us pleasure. But it also helps us learn about the things around us. For instance, we learn that a rough piece of wood may give us splinters, whereas a smooth one will not. A metal chair that has been sitting in the sun will feel quite hot, and is not going to be a pleasant place to sit.

Our skin is able to perceive all these different sensations because it has specialized cells, called sensory cells, that sense pressure, heat, or cold. Some sensory cells notice when the skin is getting damaged—a

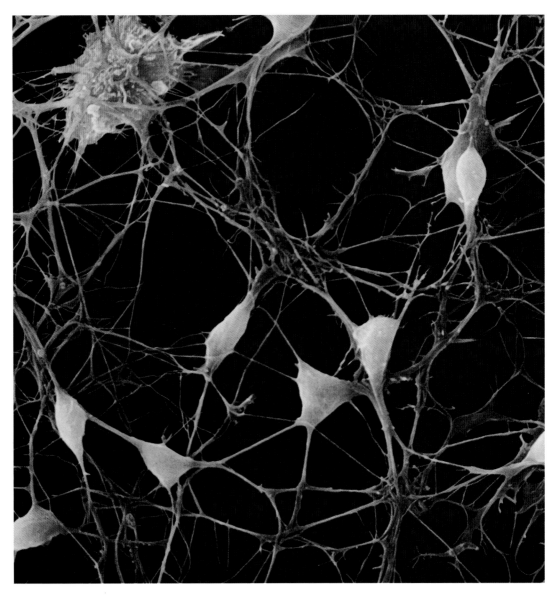

A large and complex network of nerve cells sends and receives sensory messages from different parts of the body. These messages are carried to and from the brain and spinal cord.

sensation we call pain. Each of the sensory cells is connected with nerves that carry signals to the brain about what is happening on the body's surface.

CONTROLLING BODY TEMPERATURE

The internal organs of the human body must stay near the temperature of about 98.6 degrees Fahrenheit (37 degrees Celsius) to stay alive. If the body's inner temperature gets a few degrees cooler or hotter, cells do not work properly. Fortunately, the body has many ways of keeping itself just the right temperature. The skin has a leading role.

Everybody has experienced the sensation of sweating when it is hot out, after exercising, or when you are sick. This is the skin's sweat glands at work, helping to keep the body from getting too hot inside. Sweat glands release warm moisture onto the body's surface. The moisture evaporates,

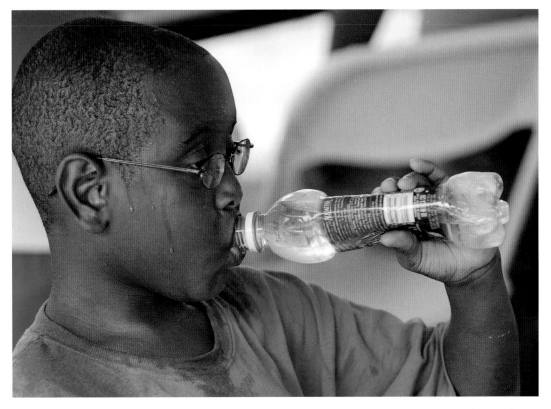

In most cases, sweating is a sign that your body is trying to cool down. When you sweat a lot you lose important body fluids, so you should be sure to drink a lot of fluids to make up for the loss.

leaving the body cooler. The brain is in charge of this process. It sends signals, through nerves, to the sweat glands when the body is getting too hot. The brain also sends signals when a person is fearful, stressed, injured, or in pain, which turns skin "clammy" (cool and damp).

Skin also helps your deeper regions stay warm when it is cold out. In very cold weather, blood vessels in the skin narrow, so that less blood travels through them. This keeps blood from getting chilled. With less blood coming to them, though, the hands, feet, nose, and ears get cold. Still, they get enough blood to stay alive—except in very cold weather, when skin cells can actually freeze and die, which is called frostbite.

Unprotected skin can be damaged by very cold weather.

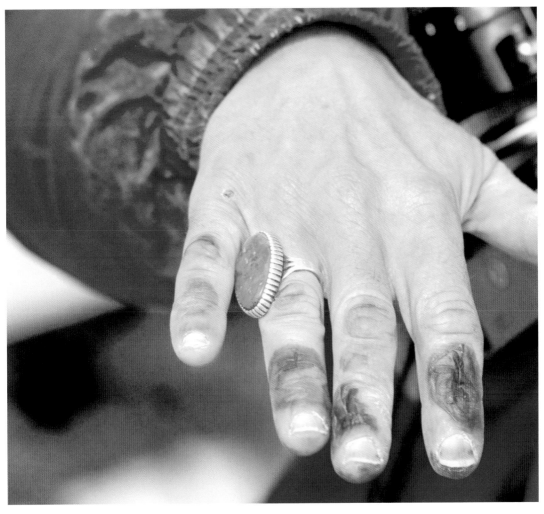

This woman has frostbite on her fingers because she did not protect her skin from the freezing Antarctic temperatures. The skin has turned dark because the skin cells are dying. Medical treatment may help her heal properly. If a person's frostbite is very serious, amputation—cutting off body parts—may be necessary.

RUNNING SMOOTHLY

Each of these many functions of the skin are necessary for good health. If any one of these tasks did not work properly, the whole body would suffer. Fortunately, the skin is very sturdy. Sometimes, though, it gets damaged or causes problems for the rest of the body.

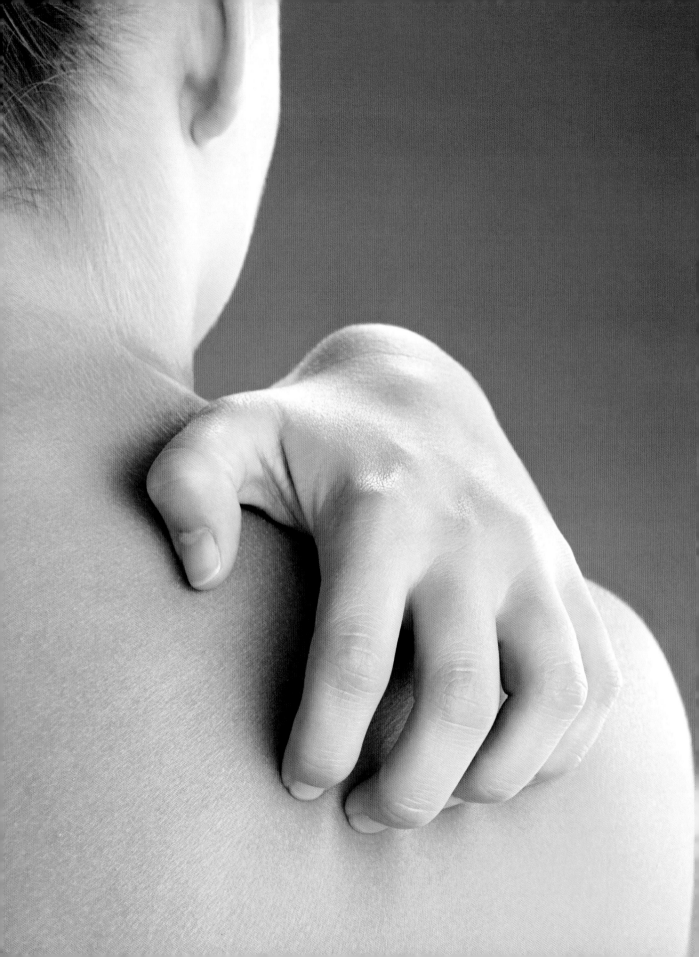

4

Problems with the Skin

For most people, it would be hard to get through even a few weeks without some minor injury to the skin. Bruises, blisters, splinters, scrapes, and cuts are common injuries suffered by the skin. The skin also can become infected by germs and irritated by chemicals and allergies. Some skin problems are minor and easily fixed. Others, however, may be serious.

SKIN RASHES AND ALLERGIES

How can the slightest caress of a plant leaf turn skin red, blistery, and horribly itchy? If somebody is allergic to poison ivy or poison oak, that

Itchiness can be a symptom of a number skin problems. But it can also mean that your skin is dry and needs moisturizing.

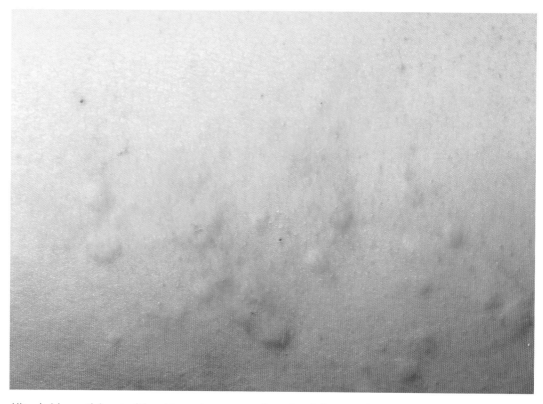

Allergic hives stick out of the skin and may sometimes be pink or red. Scratching hives may temporarily relieve the itchiness, but breaking open the skin can lead to infections and other problems.

is what happens. Many people have this skin reaction—called rashes or hives—to the oils in the plant's leaves, stems, and even its roots. But the culprit is not the plant since the oil does not damage the skin. A nonallergic person can handle the plant and have no reaction at all. The problem is hyperactive immune cells in the skin. The cells try to get rid of the oil, as though it were a dangerous microorganism. The red, blistery, itchy skin is a result of the immune cells' germ-fighting chemicals. Some people have such a strong reaction that they need medication to settle the immune cells down, ease the itchiness and pain, and stop the skin damage.

Other common things that trigger skin reactions are perfumes and colorings in soaps and skin lotions, metals, and chemical residues in manmade fabrics. Skin rashes can also show up if a person is allergic to a food or medications. In these cases, the allergens are swallowed and then carried to the skin in the bloodstream.

However, not all rashes are caused by allergies. Some people react to very hot or very cold weather with a skin rash. Even stress and nervousness can trigger a rash for some people.

Someone who has skin rashes repeatedly is said to have eczema. Medications can help with eczema by toning down the immune system's reaction and bring great relief to the itching. Still, it is important to search for the cause of the rash, because it might be prevented. If it is caused by an allergy, it may be

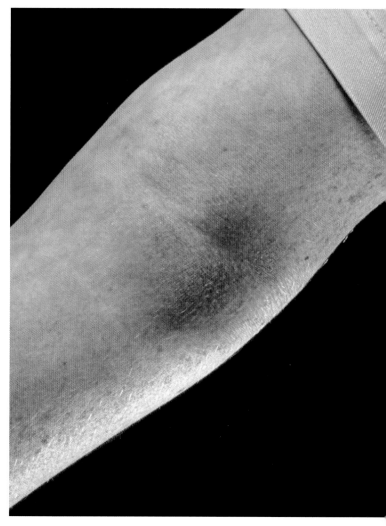

Eczema—shown here on the inside of this person's elbow— is often present in areas where the skin gets very irritated by a lot of sweat.

something as ordinary as a particular brand of laundry detergent (which lingers in clothing) or a particular food. If so, avoiding such a thing to prevent the rashes could be easy. Rashes that do not go away after a while or rashes with unknown causes should be examined by a doctor.

SKIN INFECTIONS

A skin infection means that bacteria, viruses, fungi, yeast, or other microorganisms have settled into the skin's layers. Redness, swelling, itchiness, and pain are signs that the immune system is fighting an infection. In addition, there may be pus (collections of immune cells), weeping (moisture leaking from areas of damaged skin), and changes in skin color at the site of infection.

Skin infections usually go away in a few days or weeks. But a mild infection can become very serious if the skin's immune cells are not able to destroy the microorganisms fast enough. That can happen because there are just too many invaders, or because they are especially virulent (powerfully damaging). You may have read about the rare cases of "flesh-eating bacteria," which rapidly destroy cells around them if they get into a cut or scrape. Within a day, these bacteria can kill large areas of skin and underlying muscle. Medical attention is essential to stop to the damage.

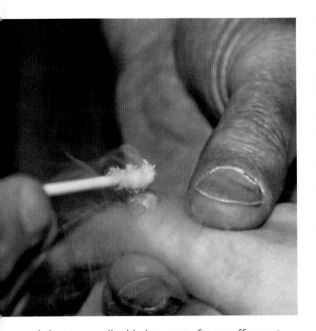

A doctor uses liquid nitrogen to freeze off a wart.

Warts

Warts are small bumps on the skin where particular viruses have settled. The viruses get inside skin cells and cause them to multiply (make copies of themselves), slowly growing into a small bump. Warts are mostly just annoying, but sometimes they become plentiful and large, which can be uncomfortable and embarrassing. Liquid medicines sold at the pharmacy can get rid of them, though it may take weeks. Doctors can remove warts speedily with very cold liquid or a laser. Before trying to treat any sort of wart-like skin growth, you should have it examined by a medical professional. This will ensure that you do not do more damage to your skin.

Fungus

Skin-loving fungus are the culprits behind ringworm, a skin infection once thought to be caused by a worm. (The marks on the skin caused by ringworm look like red or pink rings.) Microscopic fungus can live on dead skin cells in places that are warm and moist, such as folds of skin or between the toes. Athlete's foot is a fungus infection on the skin around and between the toes. Fungal infections can also affect places like the groin region around the genitals. The diaper rash that babies can get is often partly caused by fungal growth. Nails can also be affected by certain types of fungus. Infected nails are often discolored, brittle, and may grow unevenly.

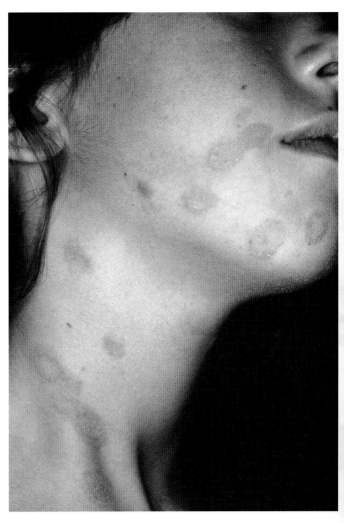

These pink marks are caused by a ringworm infection. Special antifungal medications can be used to treat the infection.

Fungal infections can be passed from person to person by touching infected skin or by handling things, such as shoes or clothing, that have recently touched the infection area. Ringworm can also be passed from pets to people, too. Fortunately, skin fungus can be treated with medication.

ACNE

Teenagers who are going through puberty know about one common skin problem all too well: acne. People besides teenagers can get acne, but it is especially common in teens because puberty is when the skin's oil glands first get active. Acne is a problem with the skin's oil glands, especially those on the face, neck, chest, and back. The pores of the glands become blocked by skin cells and oil. Pores that are blocked look dark, and are called blackheads. Sometimes the blocked gland becomes infected with bacteria, and immune cells collect there to clean up the bacteria. Their activity makes a red, tender bump, called a pimple. When a lot of immune cells are at work, they are visible as a white dot.

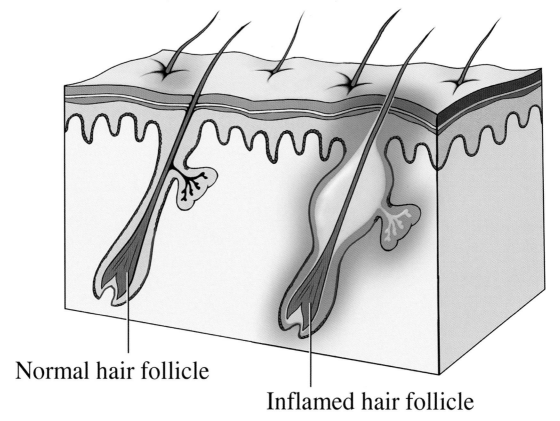

Normal hair follicle

Inflamed hair follicle

The hair follicle on the right is inflamed, or infected, because of a build up of oil. A pimple will soon form at the pore where the hair sticks out of the skin.

Problems with acne usually start when a person goes through puberty. However, adults well past puberty can also have acne problems.

Skin experts now realize that acne is caused by hormones—body chemicals—that become plentiful during puberty and remain active in adulthood. In the past, many other things have been blamed, such as greasy foods or chocolate, sweat, dirt, and makeup. (However, sweat, dirt, and makeup that block pores can worsen acne.) Frequent washing was once recommended to prevent acne, but is now thought to worsen it by irritating the skin. Pressure on the skin from helmet straps or backpacks that are worn often can also make acne worse.

Acne almost always goes away over time, though it may take years. Sometimes it becomes very serious, though, and leaves permanent scars. There are medicated lotions, soaps, and pills that a doctor can prescribe, which really help in serious cases of acne. You should never pick or pop a pimple since it can lead to a more serious skin infection and may also cause scarring.

SCARS

A scar is a mark that remains after an injury has healed. It is formed as part of a normal healing process. Skin's living cells are able to repair places where the skin has been damaged by making many copies of themselves to fill in the gap, and also by making a lot of collagen. Collagen helps fill in the wound, at the same time as the skin's cells are working to recreate the skin. Over time, the usual surface cells—the epidermis—cover over much of the injured area. But a collagen-rich area might remain for years. That is the scar. Collagen is strong, so scarred areas are actually tougher than regular skin. Sometimes the healing process gets carried away, and too much replacement skin and collagen is made. As a result, the scar overgrows the original injury site, leaving a mound of skin. That kind of scar, called a keloid, might need a doctor's skills to reduce its size. Scars from large areas of burned skin can cause trouble because they cover the wound area with sheets of tough collagen that does not stretch well. Fortunately, doctors have come up with a number of ways to reduce or repair scarring from burns, injuries, surgery, or even acne.

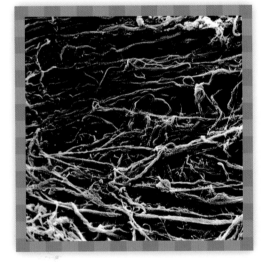

Too much collagen—shown here at nearly 8,000 times its actual size—can cause scarring.

BRUISES, BLISTERS, AND BURNS

Some common skin injuries show up as marks that usually go away. Perhaps you have noticed a bruise—the purplish mark on the skin—that shows up soon after a fall or after bumping into something. Bruises are places where blood has leaked into the dermis from injured blood vessels. Over days or weeks, the blood gets old, and it changes in color from red to green and yellow as it is gradually cleared away. The bruise may also look like it is spreading out or moving as the old blood disappears.

A blister is a raised bump where the skin has been rubbed a lot, or pinched hard. Wearing stiff new shoes, or digging a while with a shovel,

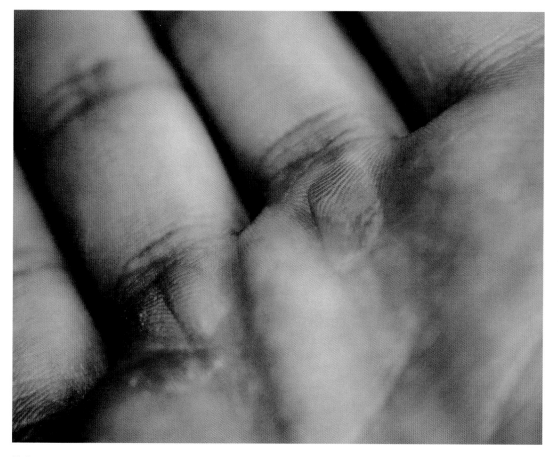

If they are not popped, blisters will usually go away on their own.

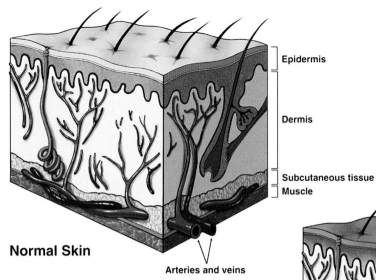

Epidermis

Dermis

Subcutaneous tissue

Muscle

Normal Skin

Arteries and veins

First-Degree Burn

• Involves top layers of epidermis only

Second-Degree Burn

• Skin blisters

• Involves all of epidermis and some of dermis

• May involve all of dermis

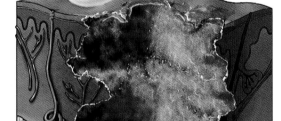

Third-Degree Burn

• May extend into deeper tissues

This illustration shows the different types of burns that can affect the skin. First-degree burns usually do not require medical treatment, but second- and third-degree burns should be seen by a doctor.

are examples of rubbing that creates blisters. Burns and skin rashes can develop blisters, too. The blister is filled with fluid, which sometimes can have blood in it. The fluid is trapped between the epidermis and dermis portions of skin, which have become separated from each other. Blisters often go away on their own. Sometimes they pop—or get rubbed open if they occur in inconvenient places. A popped blister should be cleaned and covered with a bandage. It is an open wound and needs to heal properly before an infection sets in.

Burns of the skin can be mild and nothing more than a red mark that hurts for a few hours. Moderate burns are called a first-degree burn. But burns can get much more serious. Hot liquids, stovetops, ovens, heated objects, flames, fireworks, broken electrical wires, electrical outlets, and lightning can all seriously burn the skin. Chemicals and radiation can "burn" the skin also, though in a different way from heat or electricity. A second-degree burn is one in which blisters form, and they are quite painful.

Third-degree burns are most serious, because outer layers of skin are killed or missing. And though these tend to be less painful because pain nerves are killed, too, the body is exposed to bacteria that might cause infection. Plus, anybody who has third-degree burns over more than about 15 percent of their skin is in danger of losing moisture by evaporation. Good medical care keeps bacteria out, and moisture in, as new skin cells gradually replace the missing ones. Skin grafting, which patches the burn with skin pieces from elsewhere on the patient's body, may be necessary for large burns. In recent years, doctors have learned to "grow" layers of cells in the laboratory, using small samples of the burn patient's own skin.

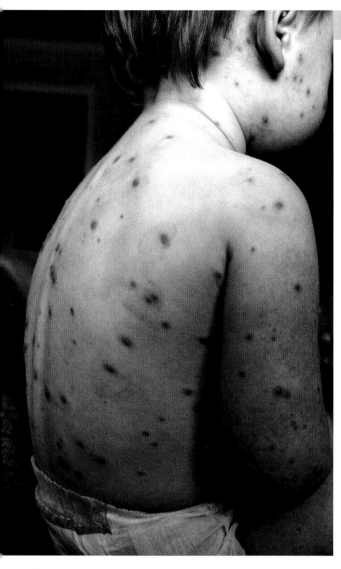

The spots and bumps from chicken pox are usually very itchy. Luckily, medication like calamine lotion can help soothe the itchy skin while it heals and the virus runs its course.

MEASLES AND POX

Some of the best known skin problems are due to infections that start elsewhere in the body. Measles and chicken pox are common examples. Each is caused by viruses that usually infect the mouth and throat first. Days or weeks later, the viruses spread to other areas by way of the bloodstream. When the viruses get to the skin, blistery, itchy spots begin to show up—often hundreds of them—as the skin's immune cells get busy attacking the invaders. Fever, chills, cough, and extreme tiredness (fatigue) are also common with these illnesses.

Chicken pox, also known as varicella, is caused by a virus. A lot of people who get chicken pox recover just fine. But some people can get very sick, and in the United States, about a hundred people die of it each year—mostly infants and the elderly. There is no cure for the virus, but the symptoms—the itchiness and pain—can be treated with medication.

Measles, also called rubeola, is due to a different virus called paramyxovirus. The measles virus can cause serious injury to the brain and spinal cord, which can be deadly. A different kind of measles, called rubella or German measles, is caused by the rubella virus. That illness is especially dangerous for a fetus (developing baby inside its mother) if the mother gets infected with the virus, because the virus can get into the fetus from the mother and cause serious deformities.

Chicken pox and both kinds of measles are very contagious. That means they can be spread easily from person to person by coughing, sneezing, or sharing drinking glasses or eating utensils, which spreads viruses that are in the mouth and throat. Because they are so contagious, young children in the United States are vaccinated to prevent them from getting sick with chicken pox or measles (both the rubeola and rubella types). But worldwide, millions of people still get these illnesses and die of them. In the 1990s, about a million people died each year of measles, mostly in developing countries in Africa, Asia, India, and the Middle East. In fact, measles was among the top ten causes of death among children worldwide. Vaccinations for children in these areas are now starting to bring the number of cases down.

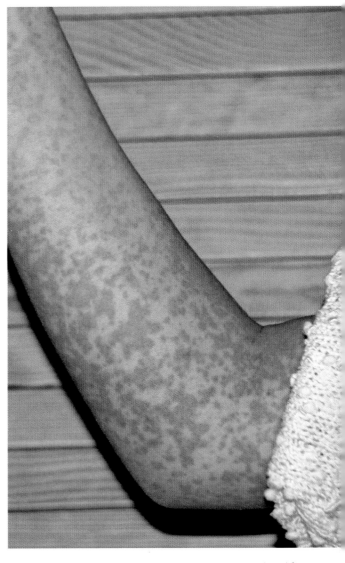

The pink rash on this girl's arm is caused by measles. After the body has fought off the virus, the rash will go away and the skin should return to normal.

SKIN CANCER

Skin stops the Sun's UV radiation from getting deeper into the body, where it could damage vital organs. But the cells in the skin can suffer damage because of UV exposure. That damage causes them to be mutated, meaning that they behave abnormally. The abnormal cells can start making huge numbers of additional abnormal cells, which show up as unusual bumps and markings on the skin. The cells can also travel out of the skin and settle in the lungs, heart, brain, or other important organs, interfering with normal activity, and eventually killing the person. This series of events describes skin cancer—the most common kind of cancer in the United States.

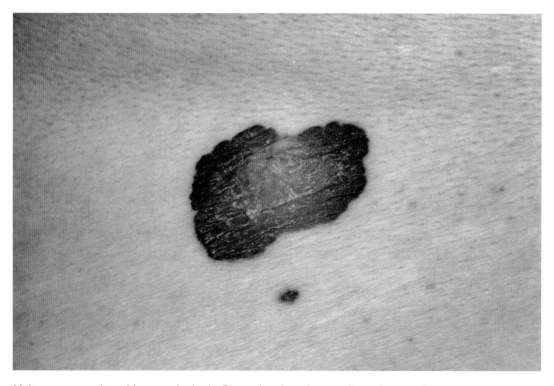

Moles are natural markings on the body. But moles that change shape, become larger, turn a darker color, or start to bleed should be examined by a doctor. These symptoms are often a sign of skin cancer.

In most cases of skin cancer, it is the keratinocytes of the epidermis that are mutated. Those cells do not tend to spread very fast, and often a doctor can remove the cancer cells before much damage is done. But melanocytes are more dangerous when they mutate. These mutated cells spread more rapidly to vital organs. Cancer caused by mutated melanocytes is called melanoma.

Cancer experts think that nine out of ten cases of skin cancer are caused by too much UV radiation. Getting just a few bad sunburns with blisters in one's lifetime increases the chance of getting skin cancer. Health experts are especially worried about light-skinned people who go to tanning salons to lay under special lights that emit UV radiation. People who go to tanning salons get the melanoma form of skin cancer—the deadliest—almost twice as often as other people. And they get other kinds of skin cancer two or three times more often.

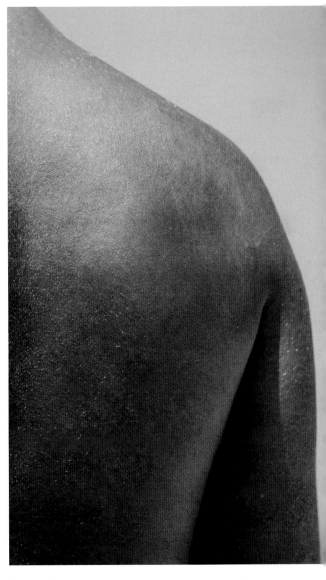

Too much Sun exposure not only causes painful sunburn, but it can also damage your skin cells and cause skin cancer.

Anybody can get skin cancer, regardless of skin color. Usually it shows up in middle age, though sometimes it appears sooner. If cancer is discovered early in the disease process, it can be stopped. That is why it is important, especially for adults, to know one's moles, freckles, and other

Doctors who specialize in skin problems—called dermatologists—can use special equipment that helps them examine moles and other skin marks. Catching a cancerous mole in its early stages can help make cancer treatments more successful.

colored markings. Any of those that begins to look different than usual, and any new pigmented markings that show up, should be checked right away by a doctor who recognizes signs of early skin cancer.

Taking care of your skin and making note of changes is the best way to prevent many skin conditions.

SKIN COLOR CLUES

A change in skin color can be a clue that something is wrong deeper in the body. Sometimes skin (and whites of the eyes) look oddly yellow. This problem is called jaundice, and it happens when the liver is infected or injured. Newborn babies can get jaundice, too, if their livers are not quite mature yet. Jaundice happens because the liver is not keeping up with its job of removing waste materials from the bloodstream. Among those materials is a yellowish pigment from old, broken blood cells.

Another color clue from the skin is when it suddenly turns bluish. This happens when the blood in its vessels is not carrying enough oxygen. Without oxygen, blood turns purplish, and skin, including on the lips, takes on a bluish tint. Too little oxygen is very serious. It might mean there is a blockage in the lungs, or in the tubes bringing air into the lungs, such as by a piece of food or inhaled water. Or it can mean the heart is not doing well at getting blood to the lungs to pick up fresh oxygen. The skin, through its color clues, can save a person's life if someone notices and gets medical help right away.

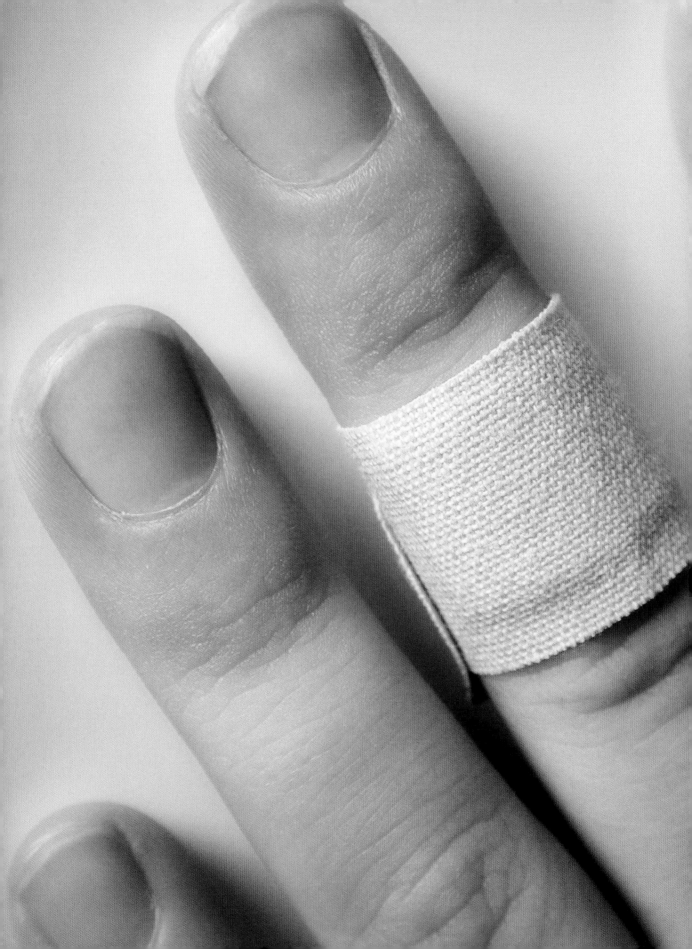

5

Caring for Your Skin

CARE FOR COMMON INJURIES

Many skin injuries are easy to care for at home. It is easy to care for minor cuts or scrapes by cleansing them with warm soapy water, then putting on a bandage that will not stick to the wound as it heals. The bandage will block germs and help protect the skin as it heals. If there is bleeding, wash the wound, then press on it with a clean cloth or bandage for several minutes before covering. But if the bleeding has not lessened, or the injury is obviously deep, get help from an adult or get to a doctor.

The simple act of putting a clean bandage on a cut or a wound can help keep you healthy. Covering the broken skin prevents dirt and germs from causing infections, while also protecting the skin while it is healing.

First aid for minor burns involves simply applying cool water or a cool cloth for several minutes. Do not use ice, butter, or grease. Burns that cover 10 percent of the body—no matter how minor the burns may be—or which blister badly or have skin burned away, require medical attention.

For animal scratches or animal bites, *always* tell an adult. If the animal is someone's pet, try to find the owner to be sure the animal has an up-to-date rabies vaccine. If it is a wild animal (including a wild dog or cat), consult a doctor immediately. Rabies is a deadly illness spread to people from animals. Other infections can also be caused by injuries from animals. Prompt medical treatment is the key to preventing serious infections.

Of course, the best way to deal with skin injuries and infections is prevention. But it would be silly to stay indoors and avoid sports and other activities just to keep your skin safe. An excellent way to both enjoy an active life and keep injury to a minimum is to continue learning about prevention and to learn about first aid, too. This information can come from a health teacher, a school nurse, a doctor's office, or even helpful sites on the Internet.

Preventing UV skin damage is the best way to fight skin cancer. When using sunblock, have a friend or relative put the lotion on your back and on other places that are hard to reach. Reapplying sunblock after swimming and sweating is also important.

SUN SMARTS

Topping the list of important things you can do for healthy skin is keeping Sun exposure to a minimum. That does not mean staying indoors all the time. You can follow these tips while enjoying the sunny outdoors:

- Wear sunscreen while outdoors for more than fifteen minutes, even on a cloudy day. UV radiation can penetrate through clouds.

- Wear sunscreen while playing in snow or boating on water. Snow and water reflect a lot of sunlight back at you.

- Choose a sunscreen with an SPF ("sun protection factor") of at least 15, and preferably 25-35.

- Look for sunscreens with the chemicals zinc oxide, PABA, or benzophenone. These chemicals are good at stopping UV radiation.

- Choose waterproof sunscreen whenever possible.

- Put sunscreen on again after swimming, and every hour or so if not swimming since the lotion rubs off or comes off with sweat.

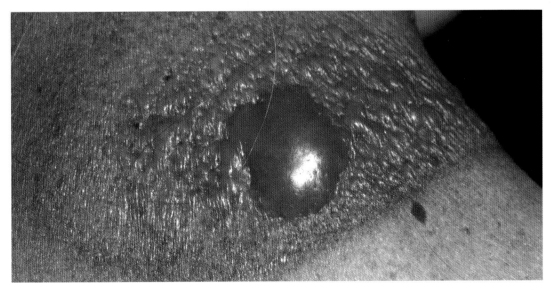

Skin that is severely sunburned may blister. When a sunburn reaches this stage it is usually a second-degree burn. A doctor can tell you how to treat the burn and help your skin heal.

- Wear a sun hat.

- Sunburns can happen under clothing if the fabric is thin. Choose tight-weave fabrics, or apply sunscreen underneath.

- If you get a sunburn with blisters, pain, or a fever, get it checked by a doctor.

- Keep babies under a year old out of the direct sun at all times. Their skin hasn't developed any of its own protection yet.

KEEPING IT CLEAN

Washing your hands is a proven way to lower your chance of getting germs and reducing your exposure to allergens. It is simple to do, and stops a lot of skin problems—and other illnesses, too. Antibacterial soaps are not necessary in most cases. Washing with regular hand soap can kill

It is a good idea to use gloves to protect your hands and nails when you are working outdoors. Dirt, germs, and other things can enter your body through open cuts or scrapes.

most germs. (However, people who work with sick people or handle and clean pets and their cages should use germ-killing liquid soap.) When washing your hands, showering, or bathing, use warm water. Hot water dries out and irritates your skin faster.

Always wash your hands with soap and warm water before you eat, especially if you will be picking the food up in your fingers. Always wash hands after visiting someone with an illness. Wash your hands after being in public places and after using public restrooms. After handling pets, be sure to wash your hands and arms.

Your fingernails are part of your skin, and they should get attention, too! A fingernail brush can help you get that hard-to-reach stuff that can collect under the nails. Every time you scratch your skin,

Using a nail brush to clean under the fingernails helps when your hands are very dirty. The dirt and germs can enter your body when you scratch an itch and break the skin.

material from under the nails can get into skin's living layers. If your fingernails are clean, you will be less likely to push germs into your skin.

After washing your hands, use a moisturizer to keep your skin moist and soft. Dry and cracked skin can lead to deeper wounds and infection. If your skin reacts to lotions with perfumes and other special ingredients, be sure to use special lotions that do not contain those substances.

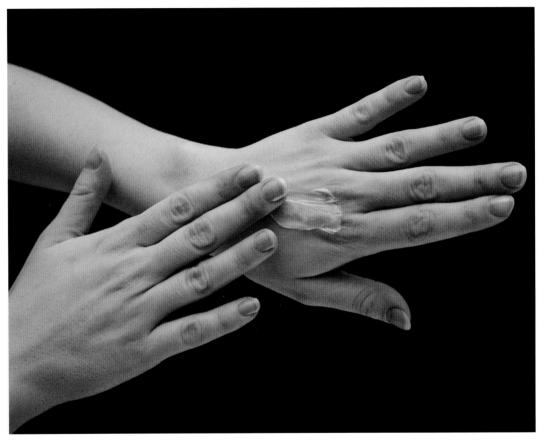

Moisturizing your skin is a good way to keep it healthy. Skin that is too dry may become itchy and is more likely to crack and break, which creates open wounds.

NOURISHMENT FROM WITHIN

The skin and hair need good nutrition, just like other parts of the body. Even though the skin's outer layers, and strands of hair, are made up of dead cells, they will be most sturdy if they come from

A healthy diet with the right amounts of fruits and vegetables is good for your skin and your general health.

cells that were once well nourished. Any living cell needs vitamins and minerals from vegetables and fruits. Fresh, or fresh-frozen, are best—lightly steamed vegetables are good, too.

It is especially important for skin that protein is part of a day's meals, because skin is made of many proteins (keratin, melanin, collagen, elastin, and more). A diet of junk food and soda has very little protein—or none at all. So daily protein in the form of grains, legumes (dried beans), lean meats, eggs, and dairy products are good for skin.

Skin has oil glands that keep it flexible, soft, and waterproof. So oils, in small quantities, are good for skin, too. Unfortunately, a lot of everyday meals, especially fast foods, are loaded with way too much oil and fats.

You should eat some fats and oils to keep your body healthy, but they should come from healthful sources, such as steamed or broiled fish or nuts and seeds.

Too much of these contribute to being overweight and lead to several diseases. So keeping oils and fats to a minimum—but not avoiding them altogether—is best for healthy skin and hair.

Besides the foods you eat, getting a good blood supply to skin and scalp is also important. After all, it is the blood that gets these food nutrients from the digestive tract to the skin. Healthy exercise gets your blood pumping through your body. It does not need to be as vigorous as soccer or basketball or rock-climbing—though those are good, too! Anything that gets your muscles going for fifteen minutes or more will make the heart pump blood around at a faster pace. Try walking, dancing, skateboarding, gardening, doing a few pushups and sit-ups before school and after, tossing a ball with a friend, or even cleaning up around the house!

Exercising and having fun outdoors is a great way to stay fit. But always remember to properly protect your skin when you are going to be out in the Sun.

READING THE CLUES

Keep an eye out for things that show up on your skin without explanation. A rash can be a sign of something minor—or something serious. For instance, in some parts of the country, a skin rash is one sign of a very serious illness, Lyme disease, caused by the bite of a tick. Medications cure the illness when taken soon enough after the bite or the rash.

If you are worried that you might have a skin problem—such as a suspicious mole or a skin infection—visit your doctor or a dermatologist to have it examined. Early detection and early treatment can help cure many problems.

Your family doctor can help you with most skin problems. If the problems require more specific treatment, you might be sent to a dermatologist—a doctor who specializes in skin problems. Remember, most things that happen to skin are normal parts of being active. But keep track of how your skin is doing, so you can get help when minor injuries are not healing well, or something shows up that you do not understand. Your skin plays a huge role in protecting your body, so you should do what you can to protect your skin.

acne—A skin problem in which oil glands get clogged and infected, especially during the teenage years when sex hormones are becoming plentiful.

allergy—A strong reaction by immune cells as they try to destroy a substance in the body that is not harmful.

bacteria—Single-celled organisms that live virtually everywhere on earth, including on human skin. Most are harmless, but some cause illnesses.

chicken pox—An illness caused by a virus, which makes a spotted skin rash.

collagen—A strong protein fiber, plentiful in the dermis.

dermatologist—A doctor who specializes in skin problems.

dermis—The deeper region of skin, below the epidermis.

eczema—Skin rashes that occur repeatedly, for a number of possible reasons.

elastin—A stretchy protein fiber, plentiful in the dermis.

epidermis—The outer layers of tightly packed skin cells. *Epi-* means "on top of."

germ—A microorganism that causes illness.

gland—A group of cells that release a substance they have made.

hair follicle—A group of cells in the dermis that makes a hair.

hives—Itchy skin rash, usually caused by allergy.

immune cells—The collection of cells throughout the body, including the skin, which get rid of substances that are not part of the body, such as germs.

infection—The presence of harmful bacteria, viruses, fungi, parasites, or other microorganisms in the body or on its skin.

keratin—A protein of which the skin's epidermis, hair, and nails are made.

keratinocyte—The type of cell in the skin that makes keratin.

measles—A group of illnesses in which viruses have settled in the body and caused a spotted skin rash.

microorganism—A tiny life-form, only visible with the microscope. Bacteria, viruses, and fungi are examples.

pores—Tiny openings in the skin through which a hair, sweat gland, or oil gland opens onto the skin's surface.

sweat—A watery liquid released onto the skin through pores, which helps cool the body.

vaccination—A shot that has bits of bacteria or viruses in it that get a person's immune system ready to fight off the same bacteria or viruses, should the germs get into the person's body later.

virus—A microscopic entity that thrives inside the cells of living things. Some viruses cause human illnesses.

Find Out More

Books

Buckmaster, Marjorie. *Skin Cancer*. New York: Marshall Cavendish Benchmark, 2007.

Farrell, Jeanette. *Invisible Enemies: Stories of Infectious Disease*. New York: Farrar, Straus and Giroux (BYR), 2005.

Hicks, Terry Allan. *Allergies*. New York: Marshall Cavendish Benchmark, 2006.

Hoffmann, Gretchen. *Chicken Pox*. New York: Marshall Cavendish Benchmark, 2008.

Simons, Rae. *For All to See: A Teen's Guide to Healthy Skin*. Broomall, PA: Mason Crest Publishers, 2005.

Turkington, Carol and Jeffery S. Dover. *The Encyclopedia of Skin and Skin Disorders*. New York: Facts on File, 2002.

SKIN

Web Sites

Human Skin—Your Gross and Cool Body
http://yucky.discovery.com/flash/body/pg000146.html

An Ounce of Prevention
http://www.cdc.gov/ncidod/op/_resources/OOP%20Brochure%2012.20.05.pdf

Skin—Kids' Health Topics
http://www.cyh.com/HealthTopics/HealthTopicDetailsKids.aspx?p=335&np=152&id=1766

Sun—Fitness for Kids and Teens
http://www.skincancer.org/protect-your-kids/sun-fitness-for-kids-and-teens.html

Sun Safety for Kids
http://www.sunsafetyforkids.org

Taking Care of Your Skin
http://www.kidshealth.org/kid/stay_healthy/body/skin_care.html

Tips for Taking Care of Your Skin
http://www.kidshealth.org/teen/your_body/take_care/skin_tips.html

74

Bibliography

"Acne." Children's Hospital, Boston. http://www.childrenshospital.org/az/Site764/mainpageS764P0.html

Marieb, Elaine N., *Human Anatomy and Physiology.* 6th ed. Redwood City, CA: Benjamin Cummings, 2003.

"Measles (Rubeola)." MedicineNet, Inc. http://www.medicinenet.com/measles_rubeola/article.htm

"Measles Database." National Institutes of Health. http://science.education.nih.gov/supplements/nih1/diseases/activities/activity5_measles-database.htm

"Necrotizing Fasciitis (Flesh-Eating Bacteria)." Healthwise, Inc. http://www.webmd.com/a-to-z-guides/Necrotizing-Fasciitis-Flesh-Eating-Bacteria-Topic-Overview

"Protecting Your Child from the Sun." American Academy of Pediatrics. http://www.aap.org/family/protectsun.htm

Rockoff, Alan. "Rash 101: Introduction to Common Skin Rashes." MedicineNet, Inc. http://www.medicinenet.com/rash/article.htm

Shiel, William C., Ed. "Burns." MedicineNet, Inc. http://www.medicinenet.com/burns/article.htm

"Skin Cancer." Skin Cancer Foundation. http://www.skincancer.org/blogsection/skin-cancer

Springhouse. *Pathophysiology Made Incredibly Easy!* 3rd ed. Philadelphia: Lippincott Williams & Wilkins, 2006.

Index

Page numbers in **boldface** are illustrations and tables.

About the Author

About the Author

Lorrie Klosterman is a science writer and educator who earned a Bachelor of Science degree from Oregon State University and a Doctoral Degree from the University of California at Berkeley, both in the field of zoology (the study of animal life, including humans). She has taught courses in human health and disease to college and nursing students for several years, and writes about health for a magazine in New York's Hudson Valley. Lorrie Klosterman has also written several health-related books for young adults. Her greatest joy comes from experiencing and learning about the amazing world of animals and plants, and sharing those experiences with others.